The Essence of Being in Court

Big Ideas for Going to Court and Representing Yourself

DAVID C. SARNACKI

This book provides useful general information. The author is not providing legal advice to any reader and is not creating any attorney-client relationship. Readers remain personally responsible for their own choices and their exercise of judgment in any legal dispute. Everyone should seek legal information and obtain specific legal advice before going to court or representing themselves.

CONTENTS

WHAT'S IMPORTANT 1

BIG IDEAS ON TAKING CONTROL 3

My Mastery of the Basics 4
    I Learn about the Law. 5
    I Truly Understand the Facts. 6
    I Develop the Internal Logic of My Argument. 7

Understanding and Managing My Expectations 8
    I Self-Empathize with My Predicament. 9
    I Eliminate Unrealistic Expectations. 10
    I Hope, Prepare & Limit Surprises. 11

Defining Objectives 12
    I Establish My Goals. 13
    I Make a Game Plan 14
    I Anticipate the "What-Ifs." 15

BIG IDEAS FOR PLANNING MY DAY IN COURT 17

My Preparation Process 18
    I Prepare Myself. 19
    I Promote Self-Confidence. 20
    I Embrace Structure. 21

The Principles and Rules 22

   I Follow the Universal Principles. 23

   I Learn the Rules of Engagement. 24

   I Act "As If." 25

Communicating My Core Message...............................27

   I Develop My Theory of the Case and My Theme.........28

   I Condense Everything Into 30-Second Messages. 29

   I Don't Waste Time. 30

BIG IDEAS FOR MY LITIGATION EVENTS 31

My Attending Presence...32

   I Listen..33

   I Act "As If." 34

   I Do Not Disturb. 35

My Presenting Presence 36

   I Focus on Problem Solving. 37

   I Am Actively Creative and Flexible. 38

   I Close Any Good Deal at Hand..................................39

My Testifying Presence 40

   I Play Fair. 41

   I Communicate My Core Message. 43

   I Make Good Memories. 44

CONFIDENT, CREDIBLE & IN CONTROL........45

ABOUT THE AUTHOR...46

Before you act, it's Prudence soberly to consider; for after Action you cannot recede without dishonour: Take the Advice of some Prudent Friend; for he who will be his own Counsellour, shall be sure to have a Fool for his Client.

William De Britaine, Humane Prudence: or, The Art by Which a Man May Raise Himself and Fortune to Grandeur (1682).

WHAT'S IMPORTANT

Whenever I enter a strange, new world, I must properly prepare. Litigation in court is one of those strange new worlds.

My preparation is what's important. I need to know what my objective is, what to expect, and how to behave. In pursuing my goals despite the many obstacles to come, I place my hope firmly in my commitment to advance preparation and real, meaningful, and impactful effort.

Since I cannot know everything, I focus my eyes on big ideas. I strive to highlight the big picture and what's important. I frame my work in three parts.

First, I take control. I do this by mastering the basics (law, facts, and logic), managing my expectations, and defining my objectives.

Second, I prepare myself. I develop a process that works for me, I abide by the principles and rules, and I communicate my core message.

Finally, I apply these concepts to the particular litigation event at hand. I give meaning, significance, and impact to my presence in any stage, whether I am attending, presenting, or testifying.

And now, my journey into this strange, new world begins.

DAVID C. SARNACKI

BIG IDEAS ON TAKING CONTROL

My Mastery of the Basics

I take control by doing the work to lay a solid foundation.

Before stepping foot in court, I must master the foundation for my position—the law, the facts, the logic. So, I commit myself to working:

- To learn some legal principles.
- To think deeply about what happened and the cold, hard facts.
- And to bring my position to life.

I Learn about the Law.

To win, I must strive to get the law applicable to my circumstances right.

Whether I search the Internet, visit a library, or consult with an attorney, I will gain some understanding of the legal principles involved in my case. I will look for the competing duties, rights, and responsibilities. I will find basic defenses, excuses, and justifications. I will note the language of the law, especially phrases that repeatedly appear. I will build around my strong points and concede any weak points without hesitation.

I Truly Understand the Facts.

I will begin by listing what I know. I will gather the documents related to my situation and see how they support the facts I know and how they supplement my firsthand knowledge. I will seek information from other sources and, when helpful, seek their cooperation in presenting the necessary facts in court.

In the absence of support from these sources, I will consider:

- whether I can compel their participation;
- whether I can expect any compelled participation to prove as fruitful as I hope; and
- whether there are other sources that might cooperate.

I Develop the Internal Logic of My Argument.

Much of the law involves deductive reasoning with a simple three-part syllogism. There are legal principles which act as the generally applicable rules. There are the particular key facts of my situation. And applying the principles to the facts should compel a conclusion.

Out of what began as the chaos of my brainstorming, I begin to create some flow of order. I will take my points and massage them into a cohesive whole. I will shape that flow to lead toward my request for relief. And I will go back over everything to see what I missed.

Understanding and Managing My Expectations

I take control by managing my expectations. This management allows me to self-empathize with my predicament, to eliminate unrealistic expectations, and—in the words of Maya Angelou—"Hoping for the best, prepared for the worst, and unsurprised by anything in between."

I Self-Empathize with My Predicament.

As I enter this strange, new world, I remind myself there is a problem to overcome. The stakes may be high, and there may be fear, especially of the unknown. Regardless, I will be prepared. I will learn the rules of this strange, new world and guide myself along the journey. I will care about my emotional journey and give myself space to feel whatever it is that I feel.

I Eliminate Unrealistic Expectations.

Understanding my needs and priorities, I ask questions. I understand that each case presents a reasonable range of outcomes, flowing from principled and reasoned decision making. I assess the proof (facts, documents, witnesses). I remind myself of the direct and indirect costs I must devote to this journey. And knowing my adversary's position and argument, I consider the risks of pursuing unlikely outcomes.

I determine my reasonable expectations, knowing there are no guaranteed outcomes. I reassure myself that since everything in this journey involves human beings, each with differing interests, everything will be dynamic and will require continual reassessment as I move forward.

I Hope, Prepare & Limit Surprises.

I let my hope for the best keep me satisfied as I prepare for the worst, limiting surprises within my power. I do not promise myself the best possible outcome, knowing my best efforts will be actively opposed by my adversary. I know it is the judge who has full control, not me. I set realistic, reasonable expectations and I take steps to achieve and hopefully exceed them.

I am honest with myself about risks, strengths, and weaknesses, as well as the expenses of litigation activities and trial. I seek to make an informed decision if the option of settling is still on the table or becomes available.

Defining Objectives

I take control by defining reasonable objectives for my journey. I create a goal for each step in the process, a game plan for how to get to my goal, and precautions for possible roadblocks and setbacks.

I Establish My Goals.

Before embarking on this journey, I have some idea of which direction I wish to travel, and which destinations might be appealing. Where do I want to be at the very end and at the conclusion of each step in the process? As Yogi Berra cautioned: "If you don't know where you are going, you might wind up someplace else." I consider what I might reasonably accomplish today. There is true value in reasonable expectations.

I Make a Game Plan.

Once I know the destinations reasonably within reach, I consider the nature of the case, my adversary, my judge, and I make a game plan.

How do I get to where I want to be? I break my journey down into segments with specific plans for each stage, like a baseball manager who plans pitchers by inning (starter, middle reliever, setup man, closer).

I focus my efforts on objectives that are achievable or within the range of reasonable outcomes. I decide what steps I need to take to achieve particular goals. I clearly define the steps and prioritize them. I prepare an action plan, arranging the steps in some logical, chronological order.

I Anticipate the "What-Ifs."

I consider what the biggest obstacles are and what could go wrong. What if . . . ?

I might not get everything I had hoped for, so I look for other outcomes within the reasonable range of principled outcomes. I consider whether to accept them if they present themselves. In other words, I have a Plan B, and I might even have an idea for a Plan C.

DAVID C. SARNACKI

BIG IDEAS FOR PLANNING MY DAY IN COURT

My Preparation Process

I will develop a process that works for me. My process includes preparing myself, promoting confidence within me, and following a structure that works for me.

I Prepare Myself.

Preparation leads to confidence, and confidence leads to the ability to perform. So, I prepare. I will strive to know:

- The case, including the critical issues with impact and meaning.
- The process, including the Rules of Procedure and the Rules of Evidence.
- The people, including the adversary, any opposing counsel, and my judge.

I Promote Self-Confidence.

The primary factor affecting my performance is my level of confidence. Whenever possible, I reduce the burdens on me. I simplify. I understand it is normal to be nervous and anxious. I accept myself as human. And I know with preparation, I can handle any problem.

I Embrace Structure.

I develop and constantly update my To-Do List, so I know what I need to address in my preparations. I listen to my own questions and concerns. I add them to my List. I strive to learn, little by little, information, tips, and strategies that will allow me to have something meaningful to share in court.

My List will include:

- Concerns I want to be sure to cover.
- Understanding where I'm at in the process and where I'm headed.
- Why the next step in the process is happening at this time.
- How I fit into that step and how I can be most helpful.
- Finding a way to accentuate the positive, highlighting my strengths.
- For any weaknesses, being gentle with myself and seeking constructive methods for improving myself.
- All logistical information about the upcoming steps: the who, what, when, where, why, and how details.
- Additional questions or concerns I have.

I look at my List with gratitude, knowing that my preparations are building my chances for success and my confidence. I can do whatever will be asked of me.

The Principles and Rules

I prepare myself by learning the principles and rules applicable to the next step, including: the universal principles, the rules of engagement, and the confidence-inducing practice of Acting "As If."

I Follow the Universal Principles.

In every step and in every context, I embrace three universal principles:

- Honesty is the best policy!
- Listen and I might learn something!
- Ignorance is bliss!

I abide in the mantra, "Always tell the truth," remembering that the truth is far easier than keeping track of mistruths. Lying causes bad outcomes and can lead to sanctions and criminal charges. It is so much simpler being myself and embracing my mistakes and choices.

If I need to apology at some point, I do it right. My components include words to the effect: (1) "What I did was wrong." (2) "I'm very sorry." (3) "It won't happen again."

I listen as events unfold, and I learn. Being in the moment and staying focused eases the process and simplifies my response.

I do not have to know everything. I can acknowledge without embarrassment: being distracted for a moment or not hearing something; not understanding something; not remembering something; not wanting to speculate or guess. I can challenge bad assumptions, adjectives and adverbs with absolutes, and conclusory words critical of my actions.

I Learn the Rules of Engagement.

Understanding the rules of the game enhances performance. I remind myself of the three big rules:

- Take Your Time!
- Information is power!
- K.I.S.S.!

Mistakes increase when I am in a hurry. There rarely is any need to rush. I prepare ahead of time so I can take my time. I want to do things right the first time.

Information is power, and timing is everything. There will be times when I must disclose certain information. At other times, there will be strategic choices to be made on the timing of disclosure (e.g., not disclosing my bottom line in settlement negotiations too early). I will understand the context of where I am in the litigation process and how my strategy may dictate keeping silent about certain matters at this moment and speaking about other matters.

Keeping it simple—the K.I.S.S. principle—almost always helps. I will understand what my role at each step in the process is, what my role is not, and how to stay in my lane. Whenever I do speak, I also listen and understand. And I tell the truth in the shortest, most direct route.

I Act "As If."

I am empowered by knowing my specific role at each particular moment. I embrace the concept of Acting "As If." Regardless of how I am actually feeling, my presence communicates three specific messages, "As If":

- I care.
- I am here to help.
- I respect the process.

For present purposes, much of Acting "As If" falls under the umbrella of being professional. The judge wants respect and expects that others present will be given some respect as well. Disrespectful behavior, getting angry, acting defensive are at best distracting and at worst upsetting and counterproductive to achieving my goals. I will strive to consistently and persistently be polite, civil, and respectful, moving myself into the being professional club.

I will redirect feelings of:

- Disrespect to: "I will show kindness even if not returned."
- Anger to: "I will show grace under pressure."
- Defensiveness to: "I will use this opportunity to share my core message."

When I act as if I care, I am here to help, and I fully respect the process, I can be confident in my role, generate empathy for my position, and become more persuasive.

As noted, the primary factor affecting my performance is the level of confidence in my ability to perform. I must remain calm enough to understand what is being asked of me in each moment. I will respond to the best of my ability. Whenever possible, I must remove burdens from my path and remove obstacles to my performance. No one needs to be perfect, and everyone makes mistakes. Me too. Hopefully, there will be some opportunity for correction, explanation, or justification.

My job is to listen as if I care, to present myself as ready and willing to help, and to respect the process and all of its participants.

Communicating My Core Message

Early on, I will define and articulate my core message. Along the journey of my case, I will strive to show the decision-maker that I have a plan, I have a compelling core message, and I am actively working to not waste time.

My core message empowers me to be efficient, to show I have a plan, and to get to the point. My core message highlights relationships, meaning, and significance. And my core message keeps me focused on what is important by eliminating what is not important.

I Develop My Theory of the Case and My Theme.

My core message centers on my theory of the case and a corresponding theme. It helps me to: facilitate a unity of purpose; keep control by focusing on the compelling features of my position; and promote my communication of the core message.

A simple overall theory is my guiding light throughout the journey. My theory will show what happened, why it happened, and why my requested relief is the right thing to do. My theme will provide a compelling moral authority for my theory, like a headline that summarizes the right thing to do, a well-known proverb, or the moral of the story.

Ideally, I synthesize (1) my goal, (2) the judge's needs and values, and (3) my factual support. My goal is to move: first to awareness of the problem; then to appreciation of the equities; and finally, to the action that remedies or avoids the injustice. The judge treasures: effective problem solving; a fair and efficient process; and a just outcome. My factual support attempts to fuse these interests together through: super short stories; statistics with context and meaning; and sound bites with my theme.

I Condense Everything Into 30-Second Messages.

For any talking point I have within my core message, I condense the talking point into a 30-second message. These messages:

- Hit the heart of the matter.
- Start with some type of hook and end with some type of ask (a specific request).
- Allow for telescoping into deeper levels of 30-second messages and back out to the main point.

I plan for two-sided argumentation. Good court-related argumentation is two-sided; it includes both The Why Not and The Why. My arguments will be structured to include and refute the adversary's argument. I do not need a sophisticated structure or all the nuanced details, but I must plan to explain, simply, the basics of:

- What the adversary's theory is and why it does not work [The Why Not].
- What my theory is and why it does work [The Why].
- The certainty of truth within my core message.

I Don't Waste Time.

Time in court is a precious commodity. There is a penalty to be paid for wasting it, so I strive for efficiency.

The judge will limit the allocated time based on three standards:

- Will it advance the inquiry?
- Will it be helpful?
- Is it likely to generate a 3-ring circus?

I advance the inquiry. Using the power of confidence, I know I have something worth saying. I have prepared my core message, and now I am here to share it. I will say it and show it without wasting time.

I am helpful. There are lingering questions. I have something important to contribute to resolving those questions. And I know which specific question is here at hand.

I do not create 3-ring circuses. Enough said.

BIG IDEAS FOR MY LITIGATION EVENTS

My Attending Presence

When I am attending a routine litigation event but am not expected to present or testify (such as a scheduling conference), I am like an extra in a movie. I demonstrate my presence by listening, acting "As If," and not disturbing.

I Listen.

When I listen, I learn. I will understand more about how events are unfolding. My focus will ease me into the process. I will be prepared to shift into a different role (presenting or testifying) if needed. I will become educated by the developments unfolding and better positioned to make good decisions if necessary.

I Act "As If."

When not occupying the space of the lead or supporting actor, I show: I care; I am available to help if needed; and I respect every step in the process. I project confidence in the presence of my adversary. I show only my calm belief that this will all work out well for me.

I Do Not Disturb.

I will be prepared for my courtroom appearances, and I will not hinder the process with disrespect, anger, or defensiveness. I will dress appropriately. I will direct my eye contact to the decision-maker, and I will use my comfortably upright posture when standing and sitting to show confidence.

If I can, I will visit the courtroom and become familiar with where I will be spending some time. I act knowing that the decision-maker is always watching. I avoid whispering comments beneath my breath, interrupting, or creating distractions while court is in session.

My Presenting Presence

When I will present information at a litigation event (such as a mediation or 4-way conference), I will act as a helpful guide in my role of presenter. Like an actor-director, I demonstrate my presence by focusing on problem solving, being creative and flexible, and, when possible, closing a good deal.

I Focus on Problem Solving.

Whenever I present information, I do so in service of the goal of solving problems. My problem solving starts with information sharing, which builds trust, identifies the range for options to discuss, and facilitates initial agreements allowing for further agreements. I may feel my emotions and the historical conflict without being controlled by them. There is work to do, and I will stay focused on problem solving.

I Am Actively Creative and Flexible.

At these litigation events, I am the key presenter of information in support of my position. I am the director. I will develop the boundaries for topics to be shared. I will work well with everyone to think about the problem, the options for addressing it, and what fairness dictates.

I Close Any Good Deal at Hand.

Knowing my specific goal for today's event, I consider the benefits of a good but imperfect deal (the proverbial bird-in-the-hand) and the costs of giving up a good deal. Brainstorming in advance of the actual event, I consider:

- When will I know that an opportunity to settle has arisen?
- What circumstances will make the timing right for me to make a proposal?
- How will I know that a given solution is good enough under all the circumstances?
- How will I evaluate the costs, risks, and benefits from both sides (of accepting a good deal and of rejecting a bad deal)?

My Testifying Presence

When I will be testifying (in a deposition or in the courtroom), I need to undertake the role of communicator. Like actors in the leading role, I plan to shine for brief moments, adding meaning to events and making an impact on the case with my core message. I will keep focused on playing fair, communicating my core message, and making good memories.

I Play Fair.

Being respectful to the participants and the process requires fair play. I am testifying to be helpful to the decision-maker. My level of helpfulness should not change palpably based on who is directing the message or asking the question (me, my adversary, or the judge). At all times, my answers will fairly meet the substance of the questions, without evasion or misdirection. On direct examination, I will be credible, giving simple, straight testimony. On cross examination, I will be credible, not trying to "win the case" with each answer. Errors and mistakes will be acknowledged. And my overall impression will be one of accuracy and authenticity.

I will follow three basic rules:

- Tell the truth.
- Listen to the question, making sure I understand it.
- Just answer the question—with the shortest, correct answer.

I may challenge questions with poor paraphrasing of my prior answers, bad assumptions, adjectives and adverbs with absolutes, and the like. From time to time, I can give short, correct answers like: "I don't understand the question"; "I don't remember"; "I don't know and don't want to speculate or guess"; or "I am not certain enough to offer educated estimates at this time."

When I don't know, I can say: "I don't know" or "I don't know, but I will look into that and follow up." When I am not sure, I can say: "That's unclear, but here's what I do know" or "I believe ___ is one who might know the answer." When I am being asked for speculation, I can say: "I can't speculate" or "I can't speculate, but here's what I do know." When my words are being unfairly paraphrased, I can say: "I wouldn't use that word" or "I wouldn't say that, but I would say . . . ."

I Communicate My Core Message.

Being persuasive requires knowing my core message and taking advantage of any opportunity to communicate it. My testimony will show what really happened, why it happened, and why my requested relief remedies a wrong.

My core message will serve as my home base. For most questions, I will simply answer—shortest, correct answer. When appropriately communicating the core message, I can transition by saying "Keep in mind" or "More importantly," followed by the message (why the adversary is wrong or why I am right).

In preparing to testify, I consider using a process like this:

- In a conversational style, I answer basic questions that I anticipate, assessing the strengths and weaknesses in my answers and my ability to get to the point.

- To relieve any anxiety and to build my confidence, I accentuate the positive. I am gentle with my self-critique. For those areas in which I sense difficulty or weakness, I tell myself, "Good; now let me try . . . ."

- I brainstorm potential areas of cross examination. I consider how best to handle those matters to ensure the decision-maker is not misled, again accentuating the positive and being gentle with myself.

- I review documents and exhibits, especially any of my prior statements and the exhibits I wish to admit into evidence.

I Make Good Memories.

If I will be making memories one way or another, why not make them good, positive memories? Persuasion flows from testimony with impact. Good general points are multiplied for impact when conclusory comments are broken down into bite-sized chunks describing events, qualities, skills, and the like. Coming back to *why* and *how* my adversary is wrong and *why* and *how* I am right should reoccur at regular intervals.

Throughout, I need to take my time. I will pause before answering. I will control the pace to stay on message. I will separate the substance of the actual question from my adversary's emotional or nonverbal mannerisms. I will remain calm and respond to the substance. If the questioner seems hostile, I ignore the tone, and rewrite the question in my head without the attitude. If the questioner acts friendly, I remind myself to be cautious, knowing the questioner is not looking out for me. I just answer the question and then stop. I get comfortable with silence. And I breathe.

When I am calm, I increase my chances of understanding the actual question and responding to the best of my ability. I speak clearly and keep the volume up so the decision-maker can hear with ease. I use good eye contact and natural gestures.

CONFIDENT, CREDIBLE & IN CONTROL

When I shape my case effectively using big ideas, I walk into court confident, credible, and in control. As I encounter a significant litigation event, I know I am prepared. I know what my objective is, what to expect, and how to behave. I rest assured that my advance preparation will serve me well and lead to reasonable outcomes for my case. When I walk out of court, I am proud of how I handled myself and satisfied with my efforts to achieve my goal in a strange new world.

ABOUT THE AUTHOR

David C. Sarnacki has published hundreds of works on law-related topics, been awarded a Commendation by the Northwestern University Medill School of Journalism for a monthly column in Grand Rapids Parent Magazine, and been cited as an authority by the United States Supreme Court in *Winston v. Lee*, 470 U.S. 753 (1985).

A frequent commentator on trial advocacy, family law, and mediation, Dave has served on the faculties of the National Institute of Trial Advocacy/Hofstra University School of Law, U.S. Attorney General's Advocacy Institute, Davenport University, and Michigan's ICLE. He has been selected as one of "The Best Lawyers in America" and designated a "Michigan Super Lawyer." And Dave has served as chairperson of the State Bar of Michigan's Family Law (2006-2007), Litigation (2000-2001), and Law Practice Management (1995-1996) Sections.

In addition to **The Essence of Being in Court**, Dave is the author of **A Visual Refresher Course on Expert Testimony** (2020), **A Visual Refresher Course on Courtroom Persuasion** (2021), and his collection of poetry, **Cry, Smile, Wonder: poems** (2018).

Mostly, Dave enjoys family and friends, venturing into creative endeavors, and generally trying to go about doing some good. He has been blessed in his life by Bridget, their five extraordinary children and growing families, and his most loving and wonderful parents and in-laws.

Visit Dave at: DavidSarnacki.com.

◆ *APPRECIATED* ◆

Honest Reader Reviews About This Book

The Essence of Being in Court

Big Ideas for Going to Court and Representing Yourself

◆*ALSO AVAILABLE* ◆

A Visual Refresher Course On Courtroom Persuasion

and

A Visual Refresher Course On Expert Testimony

◆ *By David C. Sarnacki* ◆